Personal Magnetism In Business

Hashnu O. Hara

Kessinger Publishing's Rare Reprints

Thousands of Scarce and Hard-to-Find Books on These and other Subjects!

- Americana
- Ancient Mysteries
- Animals
- Anthropology
- Architecture
- Arts
- Astrology
- Bibliographies
- Biographies & Memoirs
- Body, Mind & Spirit
- Business & Investing
- Children & Young Adult
- Collectibles
- Comparative Religions
- Crafts & Hobbies
- Earth Sciences
- Education
- Ephemera
- Fiction
- Folklore
- Geography
- Health & Diet
- History
- Hobbies & Leisure
- Humor
- Illustrated Books
- Language & Culture
- Law
- Life Sciences
- Literature
- Medicine & Pharmacy
- Metaphysical
- Music
- Mystery & Crime
- Mythology
- Natural History
- Outdoor & Nature
- Philosophy
- Poetry
- Political Science
- Science
- Psychiatry & Psychology
- Reference
- Religion & Spiritualism
- Rhetoric
- Sacred Books
- Science Fiction
- Science & Technology
- Self-Help
- Social Sciences
- Symbolism
- Theatre & Drama
- Theology
- Travel & Explorations
- War & Military
- Women
- Yoga
- *Plus Much More!*

We kindly invite you to view our catalog list at:
http://www.kessinger.net

THIS ARTICLE WAS EXTRACTED FROM THE BOOK:

Concentration and the Acquirement of Personal Magnetism

BY THIS AUTHOR:

Hashnu O. Hara

ISBN 1564598810

READ MORE ABOUT THE BOOK AT OUR WEB SITE:

http://www.kessinger.net

OR ORDER THE COMPLETE
BOOK FROM YOUR FAVORITE STORE

ISBN 1564598810

Because this article has been extracted from a parent book, it may have non-pertinent text at the beginning or end of it.

LESSON VIII

PERSONAL magnetism, then, means *power*, and the ability to exert that power over people, and even to a certain extent over circumstances, because the people we influence and come in contact with go a long way towards CREATING circumstances.

The man or woman best able to exert this power belongs to what is known as the VITAL temperament.

This, when analysed, resolves itself simply into the temperament of perfect health and vitality; although it is very usual to make this temperament a matter of colouring (red, or auburn haired people, in fact), I don't find it pans out this way at all, in fact, ANY colouring may be vital, provided the person has the energy and perseverance to cultivate the vital principles; and it's purely humbug to put any hard and fast rule to this matter at all.

The one thing that *is* certain, however, is that all *want* to cultivate that temperament who are desirous of obtaining POWER, TRUE LIFE and SUCCESS. Vital means LIFE or relating to life, and the vital temperament is used to describe those people who are in a state of PERFECT MENTAL AND PHYSICAL BALANCE.

They enjoy perfect bodily and mental health, and the one is *not* developed at the expense of the other

They have clear, fresh skins, bright eyes, firm flesh, spirits buoyant, and the power of attracting other people very great. These, in a word, are the people who possess the greatest store of NATURAL *animal magnetism*.

But the great point is that one and all can take on this characteristic, and so increase their stock of magnetic and electric particles that they BECOME VITAL!

The vital temperament radiates magnetism.

The invisible currents pass off in every direction from every part of the body, and so great is the force of this subtle power, that although *invisible to the naked eye the camera can reveal it;* and the HUMAN BODY and HUMAN MIND at once feel the impression, bodily *as a thrill*, or *sensation of warmth*, mentally as an *invigorating shock* from an electric battery, or as an overpowering desire to "*go out and do something*"!

Such a temperament has the ability to influence every person (and animal) who comes in contact with him, but has a GREATER POWER THAN THIS.

He can influence those with whom he does not come into actual contact until they are drawn to him, in answer to his thought.

This man radiates his magnetic power in the spirit of UNIVERSAL LOVE. He recognises the spirit, or the love principle in everyone, shedding his power from the store-house I have described in Lesson VII. upon mankind as a whole.

The powerful magnetic rays issuing from his person draw to him, from out of the immense mass of humanity, all that can be useful to him.

He sees *within* himself the Love Spirit; he mentally sees this spirit radiating outward from his body an essence of immense force, which finds a resting place within those hearts, or upon those minds which he so lovingly recognises.

REMEMBER that the man or woman who misuses this power will surely find it turned back upon themselves to their undoing.

WHEN YOU ATTRACT PEOPLE it is because you supply something they need, something they lack; your powerful magnetism fills an empty space. This is the secret which makes one public speaker a huge success, and another a downright failure.

The one man has a great store of personal magnetism. He holds his audience enthralled, they listen to every word and are carried along by the mighty wave of his immense strength and MAGNETIC FORCE.

The other man has none. His words fall flat, his

hearers remain unmoved. Yet he may be a man of polish, of education, of rank, with the easy speech born of cultured ancestors; and the first man might be poor, uncultured, and of the people. But the first man knows his subject, believes in his power to attract, and by sheer will power carries his point.

IN BUSINESS MATTERS the same rule applies: the man of force, possessing this wonderful power of attraction, carries all before him. He is the man who can convince the unwilling (and be it said, unorganised) customer against his will. He is the man who can draw to himself success and DOLLARS in equal proportion, and can climb to the topmost rung of the ladder.

In the acquirement of this life, force applies to every grade of society and to BOTH SEXES.

The next point for consideration is how to generate the force.

To recognise your central spirit light is hardly enough; you must fan the flame, and generate fresh power, *concerning the forces you already possess*. Brain and nerve power are the secret forces. The brain is to be strengthened and developed and so are the nerves.

SELF-CONTROL is the first factor to be observed. You, sir, who cannot keep your hands still; you, madam, who are for ever patting your back hair, or pulling at your dress, or twisting your watch chain. You who start at every sound, who fidget and fume and worry over trifles, who are nervous and irritable, giving way to passion, and being but the plaything of circumstance, to you, I say, learn to control *self*, for all these mannerisms are resulting in a continuous and serious leakage of magnetism, which if used aright would enable you to COMMAND SUCCESS.

The "magnetic" people are fair with blue eyes, and pale or delicate skins. They are fidgety, nervous, often hysterical, and suffer as a rule from too great brain activity. Their mind is never at rest, they are continually worrying over trifles, and are of a cold, and often selfish temperament.

By control you can overcome these leakages, and by overcoming, stop them. So, by nerve and brain development—recognising the brain *always as the nerve centre, in connection with the ganglionic centres, at the base of the brain*—you can control the leakage and waste of magnetism, and so become magnetic.

The so called "electric" temperament, belonging to people who are generally dark in appearance, with sallow, or pale skins, having mental powers which are often sluggish, and a tendency to suffer from liver, laziness and similar complaints, requires plain, non-heating diet, very little meat—vegetarians are the healthiest; I never touch meat—regular hours, and last, but *not* least, in addition to the exercises given in a later lesson, regular mental exercise; they need arousing, and their brain needs stimulation. They need nourishing, heat-producing foods (not necessarily meat), and they also require a time when they can be *passive*, forcing themselves to either *less* brain activity, or else to concentrate on one subject only.

These two types can, however, by following the rules I shall give in subsequent lessons, become *vital* and live as they please, master of their conditions, instead of the conditions being master over them.

The object of the descriptions of the various temperaments is intended to help the student in his knowledge of life and people, and to be used practically in the development of power.

The successful man or woman is *master*, but cannot be master unless he or she has learned how to be *all things to all men*.

When you have developed your personal magnetism you also develop your power of selection to an enormous extent, and you realise at a glance which battery to use for those you come into contact with, in business or society.

Personal magnetism, once the power has been

developed, resolves itself into sympathy, the act of supplying to others elements they lack.

This you cannot supply voluntarily unless you are in a position to order and command your own forces.

Any man who has complete control over his entire physical and mental organism can hold the world enthralled in time as he enlarges his sphere of action. To the electric person you must supply electricity, stimulate their brains, probe them with questions to make them think, and they will be glad to always do your commands, because you have shown them a new side to their nature.

The magnetic people like to be soothed; some of them, too, do not care for things easily obtained; these people you must *repel*, show them the independent side of your nature, let them believe you would rather not have any dealings with them; only give in with decided reluctance.

The more you draw back, the more eager they become. Others again need persuasion—help. By mental suggestion you can make up their minds for them.

The mental rules are always as follows; dilute them, please, with three parts common sense, to one part rule or maxim. The physical rules will follow later.

You are conscious of your own strong magnetic power, and you are aware that you radiate this power, or substance, as the sun radiates light.

You have come into business intending to obtain success only, and you hold no doubt in your mind but that the other man will deal just exactly as you desire him to deal.

When dealing with people in business or society, hold your mind firmly to the power you possess, look them squarely in the face, and command them, mentally, to fulfil your desires. Think, "I am a man of organised power; I desire to carry such and such a plan into execution. Your brain is negative to mine, and I demand that you shall do so and so. I am master; I will have what I want."

You can supply this same magnetic order when writing a letter. Hold the letter in your hand, or to your forehead, and *will* that it shall come to such and such an issue.

Your magnetic battery exists within your own body; at the command of your *will* you can radiate and generate this force.

Will power is vital thought, or mind.

Magnetism, therefore, becomes a centre of communication between gross spirit or matter, and refined, or etherealised spirit or matter. Spirit is the eternal, active life principle, manifesting in all matter, as well as through the various *spheres of spirit*.

The force which moves the world, magnetism, may be represented in your mind in one word, *suggestion*, or the command of will power, ending in either the spoken word or *concentrated thought*, is the weapon you must use through life, and that as your power so you can act by suggestion upon one man, or one thousand men.